From Words to Deeds

Continuing

Reflections

on the

Role of Women

in the

Church

Committee on Women in Society and in the Church
National Conference of Catholic Bishops

United States Catholic Conference
Washington, D.C.

From Words to Deeds: Continuing Reflections on the Role of Women in the Church is a statement of the NCCB Committee on Women in Society and in the Church. It was prepared in the Secretariat for Family, Laity, Women, and Youth under the supervision of the above committee. Publication was approved by the Administrative Committee on September 15, 1998. The statement is further authorized for publication by the undersigned.

Monsignor Dennis M. Schnurr
General Secretary
NCCB/USCC

First Printing, October 1998

ISBN 1-57455-266-X

Contents

"*Let us love not in word or speech but in deed and truth.***"**

—1 JOHN 3:18

Foreword

I N THE FALL OF 1996, the Bishops' Committee on Women in Society and in the Church began to develop a statement that would build on the bishops' 1994 pastoral reflection on women, *Strengthening the Bonds of Peace,* by stressing the continuing priority of women's participation in the life of the Church. During the next two years we consulted with many women and men—clergy, religious, and laity—from all over the country. In sharing with us their comments and critiques, questions and experiences, they have enriched our work and contributed immeasurably to the present document.

In particular, we thank the members of the steering committee, who helped to identify the major issues addressed in *From Words to Deeds,* and the advisors to the Committee on Women, who generously contributed their time and expertise to this project. We also wish to recognize and thank our consultants: members and staff of diocesan women's commissions and offices; representatives of national Catholic women's organizations and lay ministerial organizations; the National Advisory Council; and staff at the National Conference of Catholic Bishops.

We are especially indebted to our brother bishops, all of whom were invited to review and comment upon a draft of the document prior to final approval. Their support and encouragement, as well as constructive critiques, were invaluable to this committee.

The development of *From Words to Deeds* began when Dolores R. Leckey, the retired executive director of the Secretariat for Family, Laity, Women, and Youth, staffed the Committee on Women. Dolores guided our work with skill, patience, and good humor. In using her many gifts, especially her gift for leadership, Dolores is truly one of those women whom this document recognizes as working "long and faithfully to promote women's roles in the family, the Church, the local community, and the world."

Most Rev. John C. Dunne
Chairman
Bishops' Committee on Women in
    Society and in the Church

Members of the committee:
Most Rev. F. Joseph Gossman
Most Rev. Richard C. Hanifen
Most Rev. Howard J. Hubbard
Most Rev. George V. Murry, SJ
Most Rev. William C. Newman
Most Rev. Gabino Zavala

Our Purposes

"**A**BOVE ALL, THE ACKNOWLEDGMENT in theory of the active and responsible presence of women in the Church must be realized in practice." This is the teaching of Pope John Paul II, expressed ten years ago in *Christifideles Laici*, his apostolic exhortation on the vocation and mission of the lay faithful.[1]

With this present statement, we bishops, the members of the Committee on Women in Society and in the Church, reaffirm that teaching. Moreover, we offer this pastoral statement to encourage all church leaders—lay, ordained, vowed religious—to accept and act upon the Church's teaching about the equality and gifts of women, their rightful place in church leadership, and the importance of collaboration between women and men. We do this so that "the salvific mission of the Church might be rendered more rich, complete, and harmonious."[2] We urge that the steady, though sometimes slow, journey from words to deeds continue and that, wherever possible, it be accelerated.

CNS

3

In this message we rely upon the inspiration of Holy Scripture. We build on a foundation of church teaching, including papal teachings and the documents of our own episcopal conference. We draw, too, from our experience as pastors who are listening to and learning from women, actively consulting them and working with them.

We present our message not only as encouragement and exhortation, but also as a witness to what has been done and can be done within the Church itself to achieve three goals. We consider them essential for promoting an increased appreciation of the dignity of women and for responding to their concerns about the life and mission of the Church. These are the goals around which we develop our statement:

- To appreciate and incorporate the gifts of women in the Church
- To appoint women to church leadership positions
- To promote collaboration between women and men in the Church

Before addressing the goals individually, it may be helpful to say something about them as a whole.

Our Perspective

I N 1994 THE NATIONAL CONFERENCE of Catholic Bishops approved a pastoral reflection on women in the Church and in society entitled *Strengthening the Bonds of Peace.* In it we considered women's gifts, leadership, and the equality of men and women. We offered that statement as one more moment in a developing dialogue. We pledged to continue the dialogue as indispensable for strengthening the bonds of peace and for cultivating the unity that the Spirit gives (Eph 4:3). This present statement represents a further implementation of *Strengthening the Bonds of Peace.* It recognizes progress already made and suggests other strategies and actions for all levels of church life.

There are many dimensions of the Church's life in which women exercise their gifts on behalf of the Gospel. Our episcopal conference continues to uphold the timeliness and critical value of being the Church in one's family, workplace, and society.[3] Within the family we call attention to and reaffirm the tremendously important role of women as wives and mothers.

While this document focuses on women's roles in church communities and institutions, especially in parish life, we recognize that many of women's gifts for ministry have been nurtured in the family. We recognize too that while the demands of these two roles—in family life and in ministry—need to be balanced, their unique partnership supports the Church's mission in both the family and the larger society.

This committee sees the work of the many women who serve in church ministry positions as a movement inspired and sustained by the Holy Spirit. We are committed to promoting and expanding that reality as shaped by our tradition and permitted by church law.

In addressing this issue, we recognize that any discussion about women's roles in the Church can evoke strong emotions. These emotions include fear, disappointment, and anger, as well as joy and hope. We have heard women speak of their satisfaction when ordained leaders recognize their gifts and skills and use them to serve the Church's mission. We have also heard women speak of their hurt and pain when ordained leaders reject or do not fully use these gifts. Some ordained leaders struggle with their own doubts and fears as they attempt to work with women as partners in ministry. They realize that their training and background may not have prepared them for this responsibility.

While recognizing these realities, we remain focused on the ultimate goal of accomplishing the saving mission given by the Lord to his Church. There are many ways to express the Church's understanding of its mission. The Second Vatican Council taught that the Church has but one intention, namely, "that the kingdom of God may come and the salvation of the human race may be accomplished."[4] This is accomplished by God's Spirit empowering us to proclaim Christ's message in word and deed. Therefore, the Church's mission is to be open to the work of the Spirit in order to bring about the transformation of the world so that all may have eternal life.

What the Church does— its mission—cannot be separated from what it is. One of the most fruitful insights drawn from the teaching of the Second Vatican Council concerns the nature of the Church as a communion of persons (*communio*) whose relationships with one another flow out of their intimate relationship with the Trinity. The Church's under-

> Concrete steps have been taken to implement *Strengthening the Bonds of Peace:*
> - The Bishops' Committee on Women has developed *Strengthening the Bonds of Peace: Parish Resource Packet* to facilitate the dialogue and reflection called for in the document. The packet includes profiles of women, a prayer service, a retreat/workshop guide, and other materials.
> - The Leadership Conference of Women Religious has identified benchmarks for evaluating efforts to make church roles more available to women ("Creating a Home," an LCWR Special Report).

standing of itself as a communion is a central theme in the teaching that has received more attention since the council. Many implications follow from this teaching. Chief among them is the dynamic connection between communion and mission. Pope John Paul II expresses it this way: "Communion gives rise to mission, and mission is accomplished in communion."[5]

Being a "communion of life, love and truth"[6] is not simply preparatory to accomplishing the Church's mission. The very living of this communion, and the striving to do so even more perfectly, is itself a part of the Church's mission. The Church shows the world the possibility of living more deeply and completely those values intrinsic to what Christ proclaimed as the reign of God. In this way, the Church's very life becomes "the instrument for the salvation of all; as the light of the world and the salt of the earth . . . sent forth into the whole world."[7] Echoing the words of our brother bishops in England and Wales, we believe that the manner in which the Church lives its common life is part of the sign it gives to the world.[8]

A deep concern for the effectiveness of the Church's mission gives direction to everything we propose in this statement. Our conviction about the need to reform continually our structures and practices, and to renew our relationships within the Church so that we become better instruments of mission, has led us to fashion this statement on the three goals named above. Each of them casts a light on structures and relationships found in our common life. Above all, each finds its rationale in the light of mission. Gifts are given for its accomplishment. Leadership is a service utilizing and directing the gifts. Collaboration is a form of leadership and a style of ministry that flows naturally from the experience of communion and, just as naturally, into a heightened awareness of mission.

Within this context, we now consider our three goals. After each goal, we list pastoral suggestions for action at the diocesan and parish levels. Many dioceses, parishes, and groups, already moving from words to deeds, have initiated actions to put into practice the Church's teaching about women's dignity and equality. In fact, many of the suggestions below are drawn from what they have told us, as well as from our own experience and prayerful reflection. We offer them to others, to help them begin to accomplish what is envisioned in our three goals.

Goal One
To Appreciate and Incorporate the Gifts of Women in the Church

There are different kinds of spiritual gifts but the same Spirit; there are different forms of service but the same Lord; there are different workings but the same God who produces all of them in everyone. To each individual the manifestation of the Spirit is given for some benefit. —1 Cor 12:4-7

SCRIPTURE TESTIFIES to the key roles that women have played in Christian history: Mary assented to becoming the mother of God (Lk 1:26-38); the woman at the well became the first missionary to the Samaritans (Jn 4:4-42); and women brought the news of the resurrection to men (Jn 20:11-18; Lk 24:1-12; Mt 28:1-10). For two thousand years women have graced church history with their holiness, courage, intellectual gifts, and works of justice and mercy.

In *Strengthening the Bonds of Peace* we stressed that the Church better fulfills its mission when it engages the gifts of all its members. We also emphasized that the diversity of women's gifts should not be feared but recognized as a sign of the Church's vitality. We acknowledge that society and the Church have not always affirmed women's gifts. Here we include natural gifts as well as special gifts, or charisms, that are bestowed by the Holy Spirit. These charisms build up the entire body of Christ and "are to be accepted with gratitude by the person who receives them and by all members of the Church as well."[9]

Gifts that women possess—for example, for leadership and organization—are not necessarily unique to women. They are, however, shaped by women's unique experience as women, an experience that influences how these gifts develop and how they are offered to society and to the Church. We accept the Holy Father's challenge to affirm these gifts, to "examine the past with courage" and to recognize women's achievements.[10]

Dorothy Day by CNS

We recognize, first, the many ways in which women have already contributed to the Church: in building up the Church in the home, especially by handing on the faith to their children; in service to the parish; in establishing and staffing Catholic schools, hospitals, and social service agencies; as leaders of the social justice, family, and pro-life movements; as leaders and staff of catechetical programs; and as administrators and members of service and charitable organizations. The gifts of such women as Elizabeth Seton, Frances Xavier Cabrini, and Catherine of Siena have indeed been recognized. Too often, however, women's contributions have gone unnoticed and undervalued. Pope John Paul II has observed: "Women's dignity has

Sr. Thea Bowman by Michael Hoyt/CNS

Rose Hawthorne by CNS

often been unacknowledged and their prerogatives misrepresented; they have often been relegated to the margins of society and even reduced to servitude."[11]

Second, in examining the past, we see how the Holy Spirit grants new gifts in response to changing historical circumstances. Women such as Dorothy Day, foundress of the Catholic Worker Movement; Sister Thea Bowman, evangelist and educator; and Rose Hawthorne, a religious who pioneered a new attitude toward death and dying, possessed gifts that were unusual—even unexpected—but nevertheless suited to their times. These women, and many like them, challenge us to welcome gifts that build up the body of Christ. In particular, we need to affirm the gifts of women of different cultures and those of younger women. *Strengthening the Bonds of Peace* pointed out that different voices and experiences help the Gospel to be proclaimed with freshness. Women from all races and ethnic backgrounds bring a heritage from which we can all learn. Their gifts, including those for prayer, worship, leadership, teaching, and organization, enrich the whole Church.

We also need to welcome the gifts of younger women. As we said in our pastoral plan for young adult ministry, *Sons and Daughters of the Light*, young adults differ significantly from previous generations.[12] Experiences such as growing up in the post-Vatican II Church, in a culture where women's and men's roles have dramatically changed, have given young adults a different perspective on Church and society. Yet they bring a deep spiritual hunger and an energy and enthusiasm that the Church cannot afford to lose. Studies indicate a "graying" of church ministry;[13] moreover, many Catholic lay movements and organizations have a membership that is aging. They often have difficulty attracting younger people. The health of both church ministry and Catholic groups impels us to reach out to young adults.

- The Diocese of Sioux City sponsors a "Speakers Bureau" that includes speakers who reflect on the historical contributions of women to the diocese, the accomplishments of present-day diocesan women, and various women's issues.
- The Women's Commission of the Archdiocese of St. Paul-Minneapolis devoted an issue of its newsletter to "Women Saints—Models and Mentors." It featured stories about canonized saints and contemporary women who can be role models for today.

PASTORAL SUGGESTIONS

1. Use existing opportunities to educate all the Christian faithful, and especially those who hold, or are preparing for, pastoral leadership posi-

tions (priests, deacons, seminarians, religious, and lay ministers) about the Church's teaching regarding women's gifts, women's equality with men, and the implications of that teaching. This can be done as part of seminaries' curricula, continuing education for priests and deacons, and adult education and formation programs. See *Strengthening the Bonds of Peace: Parish Resource Packet* for additional ideas and discussion and workshop guides.[14]

2. Ensure that the teaching on women's gifts and equality is reflected in programs and policies. Some dioceses have found women's commissions or offices to be an effective means of promoting the Church's teaching about women's equality. Others have used an existing diocesan women's organization in this effort.

3. Use a group discernment process to identify and affirm the gifts of each member of the group.

4. Explore the Church's teaching on stewardship and look for practical ways to implement it.[15] For example, hold a "Stewardship Sunday" to ascertain the talents and interests available in the parish.

5. Periodically review parish, diocesan, and organizational programs to ensure cultural and gender awareness and sensitivity.

6. When writing the history of dioceses, parishes, and organizations, be sure to include the contributions of lay and religious women. Use Women's History Month, celebrated each March, to publicize these contributions.

Many dioceses and parishes have used the 1992 U.S. bishops' statement on domestic violence, *When I Call for Help*, as a starting point for local efforts against domestic violence. Some (arch)-dioceses, such as Milwaukee, Cincinnati, Cleveland, and Youngstown, have compiled manuals of local resources. The Diocese of Sioux City produced a video, *Love Shouldn't Hurt: A Call for Action Against Domestic Violence*. Several dioceses have held workshops and in-service training sessions for pastors and parish staff.

FOR REFLECTION

What are some of your particular gifts? How do you use these gifts to help the Church fulfill its mission to the world?

FOR ACTION

Offer a word of affirmation and encouragement to women who are trying to live out the gospel message. These can be family members, co-workers, neighbors, or members of your parish. Pay particular attention to women whose gifts are sometimes overlooked, including younger women and senior women.

Goal Two
To Appoint Women to Church Leadership Positions

In the spirit of those great Christian women who have enlightened the life of the Church throughout the centuries and who have often called the Church back to her essential mission and service, I make an appeal to women of the Church today to assume new forms of leadership in service, and I appeal to all the institutions of the Church to welcome this contribution of women. —Pope John Paul II[16]

GROWING NUMBERS of educated, talented, and experienced women are changing the face of the Church and society. Within the Church, the 1983 revision of *The Code of Canon Law* and the demand for ministerial services have opened new opportunities for women, many of whom have moved into church leadership positions at the national, diocesan, and parish levels. Nationally, for example, women serve as theologians, teach on seminary faculties, and hold key positions within the bishops' conference. In dioceses, women occupy such responsible positions as school superintendents, directors of liturgy and worship, pastoral planners, catechetical leaders, directors of human resources, and directors of Catholic Charities. They serve as chief administrators of Catholic hospitals and health care systems. Positions that were once closed to women, such as chancellor and tribunal judge, are now open as a result of the revised *Code of Canon Law*. In *Strengthening the Bonds of Peace* we

noted these developments and committed ourselves to explore new ways in which women can exercise leadership in the Church. We emphasize the need to appoint women to positions that entail substantive responsibility and influence, so that the Church may reap the full benefit of their talents.

The possibilities for appointing women to leadership roles in the Church are just beginning to be explored. *The Code of Canon Law* reserves only a few offices or ecclesiastical roles to the ordained. It provides that laity can "cooperate" in the exercise of the power of governance, expands the notion of who can hold office in the Church, and allows the Church to draw ever more fully on the talents of lay women and men.[17]

The appointment of lay people to church leadership roles challenges the Church to clarify the relationship between jurisdiction and ordination. These two rich sources of empowerment for ministry have traditionally been understood to be related but separate. Clarifying their relationship will help the ordained exercise better their responsibility for the "full care of souls"[18] while competent and prepared laity use their gifts in all the positions allowed by church law. As *Strengthening the Bonds of Peace* noted:

> We need to look at alternative ways in which women can exercise leadership in the Church. We welcome this leadership, which in some ways is already a reality, and we commit ourselves to enhancing the participation of women in every possible aspect of church life. (p. 3)

In the past, we have encouraged church leaders to identify the church roles, especially leadership roles, that are open to women. We now need to shift our thinking. We assume that all roles in the Church are open to women, unless stated otherwise by canon law. The roles are open; we need to continue to identify, invite, and educate the women who can fill them.

PASTORAL SUGGESTIONS

1. Appoint qualified women to leadership and decision-making positions, as allowed by canon law.
2. Develop ways to prepare women for leadership roles in the Church:
   - Provide opportunities and resources, including scholarships, for women to acquire the education, spiritual formation, and skills needed for church leadership positions.
   - Encourage volunteers to attend workshops and conferences related to their areas of service. Provide financial assistance if needed.
   - Encourage dialogue and cooperation between dioceses and graduate schools of theology, leading to internships and field experiences at various levels of the Church for women engaged in ecclesiastical studies.
   - Establish personnel policies that will attract and retain competent women to leadership roles at the national, diocesan, and parish levels. These policies include, but are not limited to, just compensation, position descriptions, and clear and just procedures for hiring, evaluating, and terminating personnel and settling grievances.[19] Also consider policies and benefits that affect family life, such as flexible work schedules, job sharing, and family leave.

   > - The Diocese of Albany has a policy of promoting and mentoring women as key diocesan leaders. One of Albany's three chancellors is a woman.
   > - The National Council of Catholic Women (NCCW) sponsors leadership training programs at eight to ten sites around the country to assist women in discovering and sharing their gifts in their families, parish, and society.

3. Employ women as spokespersons for the local Church.
4. Offer leadership training for women so that they can more effectively carry out the Church's mission to society, for example, as legislative advocates and as community anti-violence activists.
5. Appoint an advisory committee or similar group to track progress on these suggestions and periodically evaluate the findings.

FOR REFLECTION

How can/do women exercise leadership in your diocese, parish, or movement or organization? In your experience, what helps women move into leadership positions and what hinders them?

FOR ACTION

Read the section on leadership in *Strengthening the Bonds of Peace.* Reflect on it individually or discuss it with members of your parish or small community.

Goal Three
To Promote Collaboration Between Men and Women in the Church

*The Church's pastoral ministry can be more effective
if we become true collaborators, mindful of our weaknesses,
but grateful for our gifts. Collaboration challenges us to
understand that we are, in reality, joined in
Christ's body, that we are not separate but interdependent.*

—U.S. Catholic Bishops, *Called and Gifted for the Third Millennium*

C OLLABORATION IN MINISTRY has assumed new importance since the Second Vatican Council stressed that all the baptized are called to a life of holiness and service. Women and men alike have told us that collaboration is a major issue for them. They noted the successes they had achieved as well as the difficulties, especially when people do not share the same understanding of collaboration. Here we speak of collaboration as "the working together of all the baptized, each contributing specific, personal gifts" for the good of the Church.[20]

In this section we pay special attention to collaboration between men and women. While collaboration is not simply a gender issue, we realize that it is especially important to many women, since it expresses a genuine openness to their gifts. We realize, too, that collaboration is essential if women are to have a voice in church decision-making processes. When pastors and other church leaders fail to collaborate, women are disproportionately affected since their voices are often absent from the decision-making

CNS

process. Such failures hurt women as well as the entire Church, which needs the presence and gifts of both women and men. Pope John Paul II has pointed out that the violation of women's equality also diminishes the true dignity of men.[21]

In recent years clergy and laity have focused more deliberately on collaboration, invoking the Spirit's guidance to understand the concept and to incorporate it into church policies and practices. What is needed to make this happen? We offer a few general observations, followed by practical steps to promote collaboration in the Church.

GENERAL CONSIDERATIONS

An appreciation of gifts—our own and those of others—is crucial. The Second Vatican Council teaches that the Spirit gives different gifts for the well-being of the Church and that all believers have "the right and duty to use them [their gifts] in the Church and in the world for the good of humanity and the development of the Church."[22] Collaborative ministry is rooted in baptism, based on the gifts of each believer, and connected to the mission of the Church and to its nature as *communio*.

Ecclesial communion is characterized by a diversity of vocations and states in life, of roles, ministries, and gifts. Lay Christians have a duty as good stewards to offer these gifts to the Church, while pastors have a reciprocal duty to foster them. Effective collaboration is a sign of our deepening *communio*. For the Church, collaboration is not an option; it is the way that mature Christians express their unity in Christ and work together to accomplish his mission in the world.

In *Called and Gifted for the Third Millennium* we acknowledged that collaboration is "a huge task requiring changes in patterns of reflection, behavior, and expectation among laity and clergy alike."[23] One major attitude that we need to examine is that towards authority. We state clearly that authority in the Church is primarily about service. We see authority not as a personal possession but as a gift given to the church community to foster unity and good order. Pastors are challenged to use their authority to evoke the gifts of others and to strive to eliminate the obstacles that inhibit the full use of those gifts. All the faithful are challenged to use their gifts to further Christ's mission in the world. All must participate in building the reign of God.

PRACTICAL STEPS

While collaboration is indeed a "huge task," we can identify some practical steps to promote it. First, we need to examine our own beliefs and behaviors and confront those that may hinder our ability to collaborate. Do we see collaboration as a genuine value, in which we invest time and energy? Collaboration can promote joint ownership of the mission, but it does require more time. What strengths and weaknesses do we bring? Are we willing to trust others, or do we have an excessive need for control? No one is the perfect collaborator. Personal traits, as well as education and life experiences, affect our ability to collaborate. An example is low self-esteem, which can produce the hostility and competitiveness that work against collaboration.

Charmaine Williams, director of pastoral planning and human resources for the Diocese of Fort Worth, Tex., has worked closely with the bishop to develop the diocese's collaborative structure. One program sends a small team to assist new pastors in making a smooth transition into parishes. The team helps to explain what collaborative ministry is and how women and men can work together.

In some cases, healing and reconciliation may be needed before collaboration can take place. While we have many positive experiences of women working with bishops, priests, and deacons, we also have sad experiences of misunderstandings, jealousy, and authoritarian behavior. Such experiences have led to pain and mistrust on the part of both clergy and laity. These feelings need to be acknowledged and healed before we can

- The Diocese of Saginaw has sponsored five conferences to teach participants about collaboration. The conferences, which address such topics as self-esteem and spirituality, are targeted to Hispanic women but are open to anyone, including priests and lay men.
- In the Diocese of St. Cloud, staff of the Family Life Bureau, Office of Vocations, and Permanent Diaconate meet each morning to discuss the daily workload. They begin their meetings with the Order of Christian Prayer. This has fostered a spirit of unity and a greater understanding of each other's work.

work together as partners in Christ's mission.

A second practical step involves discernment of gifts. In a collaborative effort, individual gifts must be affirmed by the group. Some groups use a discernment process that identifies the obvious and not-so-obvious gifts of the individual. This process can help individuals—clergy, religious, laity—to recognize and value gifts and talents that they might have overlooked or considered commonplace. It affirms the unique contribution that he or she makes to the common effort.

Third, this identification of gifts helps to clarify roles. Clarity about roles and responsibilities helps to avoid the "turf wars" that threaten collaboration. Convinced that their gifts are recognized and valued, people are more likely to focus on doing their own tasks well in order to achieve the group's mission. At the same time, roles must not become too rigid. Women, in particular, have been stereotyped into roles that do not allow them to exercise all their gifts. For example, women have often been expected to carry out the behind-the-scenes tasks rather than assume the more visible roles of group leadership and facilitation.

Fourth, collaboration requires certain skills, which can be learned. These skills include communication, the ability to work with groups, and the ability to deal with diversity in its various forms. Conflict resolution and management skills are also essential. People often see conflict as "unchristian" and seek to avoid it. The wise community will ensure that some of its members have the training and skills to help the group deal positively with conflict so that it becomes a means for learning and growth.

Finally, we must nurture the spiritual foundation on which collaboration rests. This means individual and group prayer, time for reflection and faith sharing, and attentive listening to the Spirit in our midst. Prayer, the sacraments, charity, and service are, in an extended sense, collaboration with God and with those whom we serve. Collaboration is much more than just a way to accomplish certain tasks. Since God calls each of us to holiness, and since we become holy in and through our relationships, collaboration is a means for becoming who God wants us to be.

PASTORAL SUGGESTIONS

1. Offer ongoing workshops, in-service days, and training opportunities for parish and diocesan staff members—clergy and laity—on the possibilities and difficulties of collaboration. Include training in conflict management and resolution skills.

2. Use inclusive language as permitted, e.g., in catechetical and religious materials and hymnals, in daily language, and in prayer and preaching.[24] Sensitive use of language helps to build a foundation for collaboration by acknowledging the presence and participation of women.

3. Identify parishes and diocesan agencies where collaboration is working well and publicize them, for example, in the diocesan newspaper.

4. Plan discussions around the changing roles of women and men and how they can work effectively in the family, parish, and wider communities. Marriage preparation is an especially appropriate time for reinforcing the value of collaboration.

5. Work to clarify the lines of authority in the parish so that the pastor, pastoral staff, pastoral and finance councils, as well as members of the parish understand what they are accountable for.

6. Periodically review and evaluate the collaborative process in dioceses and parishes.

FOR REFLECTION

What has been your own experience of collaboration in the family, the workplace, and the parish? How have the rewards and the challenges of collaboration affected your spiritual growth?

FOR ACTION

Take a personal inventory of the strengths and weaknesses that affect your ability to collaborate. What positive qualities do you bring and what attitudes and behaviors might you need to change?

Our Commitment

A S THE COMMITTEE ON WOMEN in Society and in the Church, we commit ourselves to continuing our advocacy on behalf of women. In recent years that advocacy has included statements on domestic violence and child sexual abuse in the home; a video on how to preach about domestic violence; and a colloquium to examine the meaning of Catholic feminism. We pledge to explore new ways in which we can effectively advocate on behalf of women. In particular, we will give special attention to two areas. First, heeding the Holy Father's call "to pay attention to the whole question of how women's specific gifts are nurtured, accepted, and brought to fruition in the ecclesial community,"[25] we will educate ourselves about the particular needs, concerns, and gifts of women and how women's gifts can be affirmed and incorporated into church life. Second, we will explore what new forms of church leadership may be needed for our time and take steps to ensure that women are prepared for these as well as existing leadership roles.

The committee recognizes the need to track progress on the suggestions contained in this statement. Accordingly, the committee will maintain a relationship with diocesan women's commissions and offices and national women's organizations to review progress and to hear suggestions for further action.

Conclusion

I N CHOOSING TO SPEAK again about women's gifts and leadership four years after *Strengthening the Bonds of Peace*, we stress its continuing priority. We encourage those women and men who have worked long and faithfully to promote women's roles in the family, the Church, the local community, and the world. At the same time, we use the occasion of the Jubilee Year 2000 to acknowledge past mistakes and failures to act, realizing that the joy of jubilee is based on a genuine conversion of heart.[26] In order to move from words to deeds, we need an ongoing conversion of mind and heart that leads us to undertake not only these suggested actions, but others that are inspired by the Spirit.

Our fundamental recommendation, however, is directed to each member of the Church: to examine prayerfully our own hearts and minds, to ask whether our attitudes and behaviors, our words and our deeds, promote progress on women's roles in the Church. Harsh rhetoric, simplistic and unjust labeling of others, arrogance, and an unwillingness to listen to and learn from those with a different perspective all impede progress. Our challenge—still—is to forge "the bonds of peace," to become a sign of unity, a sign of the Spirit's work among us.

We can meet this challenge only by living personally in the Spirit. We need to pray for each other, to discern how the Spirit is leading us, and to have both the humility and the fortitude to follow. Above all, we must remember that the work we do is not ours but God's—in whose name it begins, under whose guidance it continues, and in whose glory it ends.

Notes

1. John Paul II, *The Vocation and Mission of the Lay Faithful in the Church and in the World (Christifideles Laici)* (Washington, D.C.: United States Catholic Conference, 1988), no. 51.
2. *Christifideles Laici,* no. 52.
3. For example, see the U.S. bishops' statements, *Follow the Way of Love* (Washington, D.C.: United States Catholic Conference, 1994) and *Communities of Salt and Light* (Washington, D.C.: United States Catholic Conference, 1994).
4. Vatican Council II, *Pastoral Constitution on the Church in the Modern World (Gaudium et Spes),* no. 45.
5. *Christifideles Laici,* no. 32.
6. Vatican Council II, *Dogmatic Constitution on the Church (Lumen Gentium),* no. 9.
7. Ibid.
8. Bishops' Conference of England and Wales, *The Sign We Give: Report from the Working Party on Collaborative Ministry* (1995).
9. *Catechism of the Catholic Church* (Washington, D.C.: United States Catholic Conference, 1994), nos. 799-800.
10. John Paul II, *Letter to Women* (Washington, D.C.: United States Catholic Conference, 1995), no. 3.
11. Ibid.
12. National Conference of Catholic Bishops, *Sons and Daughters of the Light: A Pastoral Plan for Ministry with Young Adults* (Washington, D.C.: United States Catholic Conference, 1996).
13. National Pastoral Life Center, preliminary report to the NCCB Subcommittee on Lay Ministry, November 1997.
14. NCCB Committee on Women in Society and in the Church, *Strengthening the Bonds of Peace: Parish Resource Packet* (Washington, D.C.: United States Catholic Conference, 1996).

15. See National Conference of Catholic Bishops, *Stewardship: A Disciple's Response* (Washington, D.C.: United States Catholic Conference, 1993).

16. John Paul II, Letter to Mary Ann Glendon and the Holy See's Delegation to the Fourth World Conference on Women (August 29, 1995), in *Pope John Paul II on the Genius of Women* (Washington, D.C.: United States Catholic Conference, 1997), 62.

17. See canon 129.2. Also see canons 145 and 149 on the qualities necessary to hold office and canon 517.2, dealing with the pastoral care of parishes that do not have a resident pastor.

18. "Full care of souls" is described as the pastoral care reserved to the priest. See canon 150.

19. Consult *Just Treatment for Those Who Work for the Church* (Cincinnati: National Association of Church Personnel Administrators, 1986). Also consult *The Individual and the Institution: Strengthening Working Relationships in the Church* (Cincinnati: National Association of Church Personnel Administrators, 1994).

20. NCCB Committee on the Laity, *Gifts Unfolding: The Lay Vocation Today With Questions for Tomorrow* (Washington, D.C.: United States Catholic Conference, 1990), 49.

21. John Paul II, *On the Dignity and Vocation of Women (Mulieris Dignitatem)* (Washington, D.C.: United States Catholic Conference, 1989), no. 10.

22. Vatican Council II, *Decree on the Apostolate of the Laity (Apostolicam Actuositatem)*, no. 3.

23. National Conference of Catholic Bishops, *Called and Gifted for the Third Millennium* (Washington, D.C.: United States Catholic Conference, 1995), 18.

24. See National Conference of Catholic Bishops, *Strengthening the Bonds of Peace* (Washington, D.C.: United States Catholic Conference, 1995), 11-12.

25. Address of Pope John Paul II to Bishops from Region VI (May 21, 1998), in *Ad Limina Addresses: February 1998-October 1998* (Washington, D.C.: United States Catholic Conference, 1998), 48.

26. See John Paul II, *On the Coming of the Third Millennium (Tertio Millennio Adveniente)* (Washington, D.C.: United States Catholic Conference, 1994), no. 32.